JOUR

Big Questions

A Journey Tackling Life's Most Important Issues

Jim Bryden

O&U
Onwards & Upwards

Big Questions

Onwards and Upwards Publishers

4 The Old Smithy, London Road, Rockbeare,
EX5 2EA, United Kingdom.
www.onwardsandupwards.org

Copyright © Jim Bryden 2022

First edition, published in the United Kingdom by Onwards and Upwards Publishers (2022).

ISBN:	978-1-78815-589-2
Typeface:	Sabon LT
Editor:	Hilja Jeffery
Graphic design:	LM Graphic Design

The views and opinions expressed in this book are the author's own, and do not necessarily represent the views and opinions of Onwards and Upwards Publishers or its staff.

Endorsements

Drawing on wide reading, personal experience and biblical study, Jim Bryden invites his readers to think, pray and talk together about important questions that challenge believers today. On the fifth and final stage of his *Journey of Faith* he poses thought-provoking questions about God's relation to the created world, the reality of heaven and hell, and the role of religion in society. He then turns to more personal topics: What does it mean to 'walk with God'? How can Christians share their faith with others? Jim's Journey ends, as it began, with prayer.

Dr John Coutts M.A., B.D., Ph.D.
Formerly Senior Lecturer in Theology,
University of Greenwich

In his final book in this series, Jim Bryden considers matters that are collectively described in Christian theology as 'Last Things.' Heaven, hell, and the hereafter are dealt with alongside thoughts about the redemption of all Creation and ultimate questions on the reign of God.

As with his earlier volumes, Jim brings his own insights after long years in Christian life and ministry to the task. All this viewed through an essentially conservative evangelical lens.

Lieut-Colonel Ian Barr, B.D., M.A
Salvation Army Officer in Retirement

About the Author

As a young teenager and non-churchgoer, Jim had a Damascus Road encounter with Christ which was to lead him into ministry in The Salvation Army. He and his wife Helen were ordained and commissioned as officers in 1968 and served in Scotland, South America, Zimbabwe and England.

Always a pastor and preacher first, he's held a variety of posts as a tutor and lecturer in Bible studies and Theology at The Salvation Army's International College in London and as Training Principal in Zimbabwe.

Besides academic and pastoral responsibilities, for the last six years of active ministry he held the post of Territorial Ecumenical officer for the United Kingdom and Republic of Ireland.

He holds a Bachelor of Divinity degree (Glasgow) and a Masters in Systematic Theology from King's College London.

To Helen,
my darling wife,
and
our two children:

Sheron Kourosh
'Journeying with us'

David Bryden
1964-2009
'With the Lord'

Big Questions

Contents

Big Questions

Introduction

'BIG QUESTIONS' IS THE FIFTH AND FINAL BOOK
in the *Journey of Faith* series. I invite you to consider some
of life's most urgent questions, such as:

- Can God save his creation?
- Are heaven and hell for real?
- Will a loving God judge the world?
- Is religion all about war?

Then, on a personal note:

- Are you lost or found?
- What is it like to walk with God?

Next, to look at matters of God's sovereignty, asking:

- Is God in control?
- What is the kingdom of God?
- What is meant by God reigning?
- What matters most in life?

Lastly, a personal challenge:

- Will you share your faith with others?

Some Chapters' Opening Words

> *What make the world go round? It's more than
> love. It's God's love, grace and power.*

> *Ever since Eve caved into Satan's subtle
> temptation to eat the forbidden fruit with*

Adam, humanity and all creation has gone to rack and ruin.

In the journey of faith the ultimate destination stares us in the face. The question we all ask never goes away: what happens after we die?

After death comes judgement, a sphere where Christ will be lifted high and before whom all will acknowledge his Lordship.

Is there such a thing as a holy war?

Today, is there a street where families are not at war? Relationships flounder and fail, while moral standards cry for answers.

God rules in love and justice. Every follower is accountable to him in faithfulness to his Word and costly service to others.

In the Bible, 'eternal life' is synonymous with 'life in the kingdom of God'.

I find myself burdened again by a deep longing to reach the 'lost' with the gospel of Christ. The Lord has brought this home to me time and again.

In the Old Testament, Psalm 121 is one of the pilgrim psalms. It traces the journey of life and faith and celebrates the fact that God's guardian care provides strength and protection from any and every calamity life can throw at you.

Begin the journey tackling life's most important issues.

1

Is God in Control?

WHAT MAKES THE WORLD GO ROUND? IT'S more than love. It's God's love, grace and power. But it's so easy for humankind to feel they control everything, particularly when science or money seems to rule; or when a particular brand of political correctness replaces God's moral order and people look to celebrities and cults for answers to life's challenges.

The truth is that while the inhabitants of earth's northern hemisphere enjoy more and more 'things', we have not yet learned how to wipe away debt in the developing world or initiated effective recovery or renewal programmes for the people living there. Vast populations hover between life and death for lack of resources.

Our world might have 'shrunk' to the extent that we now live in a global village, but our appetite for power and possessions seems insatiable. While God has provided enough to go round, sins of pride, prejudice, greed and godlessness pollute and spoil our wonderful world. None of us would be here but for God. The Son of God is his agent in creation. In Hebrews we read:

> *The Son is the radiance of God's glory and the exact representation of his being, sustaining all things by his powerful word. After he had*

> *provided purification for sins, he sat down at
> the right hand of the Majesty in heaven.*
>
> *Hebrews 1:3 (NIVUK)*

Now there's a shock for experts who proudly think they're in charge and that the future of the planet and its people rests in the hands of 'saviour figures' in society.

In the face of such things, men and women appear small, frail, powerless and impotent. Scientists tell us that research on human embryos could lead to a cure for chronic conditions such as Alzheimer's or Parkinson's disease. In the UK, strict laws for a long time were in place that forbade cloning of human beings; but Parliament, in the year 2000, opened a door that might never be shut, by approving the use of human embryos in the fight against human disease. The fact that something *can* be done does not necessarily mean it *should* be done. Science without ethics – worse still, where it operates in vistas of research that fail to take cognisance of God's hand in life – could wreak havoc and destruction. God the Creator is dynamically active in what we see, and don't see, in and around us.

Authorities, scientists – or the Church, for that matter – should not think too highly of themselves. Christ Jesus alone is supreme and pre-eminent in all things. God's reflection is seen in his Son, who is 'the radiance of God's glory and exact representation of his being, sustaining all things by his powerful word'. A new Adam and a new Eve, a new creation without and within, has been made possible only through Christ's sacrificial death and resurrection. Everything else is sheer folly and foolishness – a surrender to the archenemy, Satan, who rejects God's radiance in favour of darkness and death.

How does the Son exercise his power? The answer is found in the prologue to John's Gospel:

> *Before anything else existed, there was Christ, with God. He has always been alive and is himself God. He created everything there is – nothing exists that he didn't make. Eternal life is in him, and this life gives light to all mankind. His life is the light that shines through the darkness – and the darkness can never extinguish it.*
>
> *John 1:1-5 (TLB)*

There it is, plainer than day: God's creation is realised through Christ, and Christ holds it all together.

The discovery that Saturn is a gigantic protective shield for the earth[1] does not explain away the hand of God in space and nature but only reinforces the reality of God in these spheres – observed in the wonder of survival in the face of threat of annihilation from outer space.

Stars move with precision in their celestial path, but Christ has sovereignty over all creation and is affirmed in mighty power. From the vast regions of outer space to the inner sphere of the human heart, Christ, the radiance of God, must and will reign in power and majesty.

---

[1]   https://www.dailymail.co.uk/sciencetech/article-1203405/Guardian-planets-Jupiter-Saturn-shield-Earth-catastrophic-comet-collisions.html

QUESTIONS

How do we build a better world practically and spiritually?

Pride, prejudice, possessions and power without any controls open the door to disaster. What is God's way of dealing with this?

Where does God's Son figure in relation to his Father in creation and re-creation?

2

Can God Save His Creation?

EVER SINCE EVE CAVED INTO SATAN'S SUBTLE temptation to eat the forbidden fruit with Adam, humanity and all creation has gone to rack and ruin. As we read in Genesis:

> *When the Woman saw that the tree looked like good eating and realised what she would get out of it – she'd know everything! – she took and ate the fruit and then gave some to her husband, and he ate...*
>
> *Genesis 3:6 (MSG)*

The human race has pandered to its pride, striven for knowledge as power and too readily congratulated itself on its assumption of progress. Even worse, many people today have abandoned serious belief in God – not unlike the man on a TV chat show who boasted God was an irrelevance, claiming better gods existed in the shape of money and man-made achievements. The chase for more and more money has become a marathon in which the gambling industry is frontrunner, wooing contestants to put their money where their dreams are. This might seem harmless enough, but it tempts an ever-increasing number of people, who find themselves paying the price of a habit hard to break.

Far from having their eyes opened, our first parents were blinded by their disobedience. Many people today are deceived by the Evil One into placing faith in human success. In the words of the apostle Paul, people's 'thinking became futile and their foolish hearts were darkened'[2].

Science has become the panacea of all our ills. Our expanding universe soars on wings of invincibility, leading some to confuse infinity with divinity. As the boundaries of knowledge expand, with not a little help from 'dot-com' and social media, the notion of humankind unlocking the secrets of life becomes an irresistible dream, leaving little or no room for God, unless that god happens to be man himself or man-formed fanciful notions of God. The naked truth is simply that without God the human race is as confused as an infant would be by an A-level maths exam!

The Green lobby campaigns to preserve our planet, to share its resources more justly and to live with greater respect towards nature and environment. But political unrest, lawlessness, selfish use of natural resources, financial greed, racism and religious intolerance threaten the future of our children and our very survival. The question remains: does humanity possess the will and means of guaranteeing that life on earth will continue?

I suggest to you that we have the will but none has the means. Only God can save the world and the human race. So, why does God bother with us? What lies behind his will to save, and for what purpose? It all comes down to the greatest reality known to mankind: namely, because God loves like no other, he wills to save from loss and

---

[2] Romans 1:21 (NIVUK)

destruction and draw to himself all creation, which without him has no life.

Let's take time to look on the one he favours above all else: Jesus. He is God's one and only Son, uniquely 'the way and the truth and the life'[3].

He, Christ Jesus, is the radiance of God. Is there a way to describe the Son of God? We could use the sun as a metaphor. Imagine a glorious dawn at sunrise: rays of light shattering the darkness; dazzling beauty, warm, packed with promise. Yet this symbol, magnificent and mighty as it is, fails to convey the truth of Christ who is 'the radiance of God's glory'[4]. Make no mistake, Jesus is the mirror image of God. He is the perfect portrait of his Father God unveiled before our very eyes; the visible expression of the invisible God! In the Greek, the word for 'image' (*eikon* or 'icon') means a representation, a manifestation of God.

Can we see God? Many subscribe to the view that seeing is believing. 'Show me God,' say some, 'and I'll believe.' 'Perform a miracle,' say others, 'and you'll convince me. In fact, you might see me in church.' While my wife and I served as missionaries in South America in the early 1970s, our daughter Sheron was only an infant. One day she was very frightened. 'It's all right, darling,' her mum told her warmly. 'Jesus is here.' Instantly, springing bold upright in bed, Sheron replied, 'Yes, Mummy, but I'd rather have someone with skin on!'

When Jesus was tempted he had 'skin on'.[5] The narrative provides important lessons about how to deal

---

[3] John 14:6 (NIVUK)

[4] Hebrews 1:3 (NIVUK)

[5] See Luke 4:1-13

with pride and power. We see Jesus emphatically rejecting the misuse of power by refraining from magic or the performance of miraculous acts. Recognition of the identity of Jesus as God's unique Son, and his kingdom mission to impart life and a future, could not be realised by trickery and delusion. Stones into bread might answer social deprivation; a fantastic leap from a height without a parachute would prove entertaining – with angels mobilised in a split second as an emergency rescue team! Or how about an adoring world at your feet, swayed by the spectacular, and dazzled by splendour? *No magic here, thank you!* These would all be cheap stunts doomed to failure, appealing, as they would, to the senses only and not to faith.

A deal with Satan is a deal against God and his Word. Proofs and tangible signs are not God's way – they are trying to elevate the physical above the spiritual and applaud deception in preference to integrity and truth. God alone can rescue the planet, halt the spiral threat to our civilisation and provide a safe, secure and satisfying future. Only God knows the way! We ignore this eternal truth at our peril.

QUESTIONS

In today's world many have abandoned belief in God. List and comment on significant ways to reach such people with the gospel.

_____

_____

_____

_____

_____

Why do you believe the reality of Satan must be taken seriously?

_____

_____

_____

How does God save the planet?

_____

_____

_____

3

Are Heaven and Hell for Real?

IN THE JOURNEY OF FAITH, THE ULTIMATE destination stares us in the face. The question we all ask never goes away: what happens after we die? As Christians we reject the idea that we cease to exist or are absorbed into the life of the divine, a process that robs us of our God-given individuality. Rather, death is both the end and the beginning: the end of this life and the start of another.

For those in Christ, death opens the door to heaven and to life in the eternal presence of God. A different reality meets those who choose to shut out God's Son from their lives – a terrible beginning, that more accurately may be described as the end. Though they live, they are as good as dead, for God is not present. No language could convey the torment of spending eternity without God, without love, without hope for those who refuse to acknowledge God's Son as Lord and Saviour.

Do sinners really go to hell? Yes, they do. What is hell but being locked into self-centred, destructive, devilish existence? Worst of all, it is to be cut off from God. God's grace rejected is hell's anguish accepted.[6] The bottom line is simply this: both heaven and hell are dimensions of existence entered as a result of choices made in this life. How deeply crucial it is that the right decision be made!

---

[6] See Matthew 13:49,50

When people talk about the 'immortality of the soul' this should not be confused with the 'resurrection of the body'. If there is such a thing as an 'eternal soul' then its timelessness is God-given. Nature and the natural world are 'fallen' (spiritually speaking) and on a collision course to destruction. Eternal survival derives not from the cosmos but its Creator. Life, whatever form it takes, comes from God. Nothing has a life of its own or can be placed beyond his control. Eternal life is possible purely because God, without beginning or end, is himself the source and sustainer of life. The apostle Paul drives it home:

> *The God who made the world and everything in it, this Master of sky and land, doesn't live in custom-made shrines or need the human race to run errands for him, as if he couldn't take care of himself. He makes the creatures; the creatures don't make him. Starting from scratch, he made the entire human race and made the earth hospitable, with plenty of time and space for living so we could seek after God, and not just grope around in the dark but actually find him. He doesn't play hide-and-seek with us. He's not remote; he's near.*
>
> *Acts 17:24-28 (MSG)*

The concept that we are 'naturally' immortal is not Christian but Greek. Resurrection correctly describes the Church's belief because it points to the survival of the

21

whole person and not just a part, as immortality of the soul might suggest.[7]

After death comes judgment – a sphere where Christ will be lifted high and 'every tongue acknowledge that Jesus Christ is Lord'[8]. God's way will be seen as the right way; injustices will be addressed, wrongs righted and truth will be triumphant. Believers and non-believers 'will … stand before God's judgment seat'[9]. The consequences of 'doing one's own thing', as opposed to God's, will be seen to result in alienation from God's presence. In love, God will not ignore his own righteousness by overriding the exercise of free will given to humanity.

Today, Christian thinking is dominated by the notion of the God of love to such a degree that there is a tendency to play down his wrath. As A. W. Tozer says, 'The vague and tenuous hope that God is too kind to punish the ungodly has become a deadly opiate for the consciences of millions.'[10] The fact remains that God brooks no compromise with sin; not now, not then. As Paul and the book of Isaiah so truthfully and frighteningly point out, '...the wrath of God is being revealed from heaven against all the godlessness and wickedness of people...'[11] Those who refuse God's priceless salvation continue in sin and so God will banish them to their chosen way.[12]

---

[7] See 1 Corinthians 15:42-44
[8] Philippians 2:11 (NIVUK)
[9] Romans 14:10 (NIVUK)
[10] A. W. Tozer; *The Knowledge of the Holy;* General Press (2019)
[11] Romans 1:18 (NIVUK)
[12] See Isaiah 59:2; Luke 16:19-31; Romans 2:8

'I am constantly astounded,' wrote the late Dr Billy Graham in his book *Angels: God's Secret Agents*[13], 'that God's decrees and warnings are considered so lightly in our modern world – even among Christians.' For Christ's followers, the new life begun on earth will expand to limitless depths of joy, peace and praise as they enter into that perfect union with God himself, whose word given in promise is finally brought to pass in perfect reality!

The way of faith, now shrouded in mystery, will become clear. High and above all else will be the sight of him, our Lord Jesus Christ, who died to bring life in all its fulness. What joy, what peace, what wonder where the faithful, called to be like him, will share in the fulness of his presence![14]

---

[13] Hodder and Stoughton (2004); p.101
[14] 1 John 3:2; 4:17

QUESTIONS

Christians believe that life does not die with death; instead, it continues in the glory of heaven or the curse of hell. What do you make of this?

After death comes judgment where all humanity will acknowledge Christ's divinity but only believers will share in his glory. What does this say to you?

How do you explain God's love and God's wrath as non-contradictory?

Describe the glory of heaven and its prize reward as you find it in scripture.

4

Will a Loving God Judge the World?

AFTER DEATH COMES JUDGEMENT – A SPHERE where Christ will be lifted high and before whom all will acknowledge his Lordship.

> *Therefore God exalted him to the highest place*
>> *and gave him the name that is above every name,*
> *that at the name of Jesus every knee should bow,*
>> *in heaven and on earth and under the earth,*
> *and every tongue acknowledge that Jesus Christ is Lord,*
>> *to the glory of God the Father.*
>
> *Philippians 2:9-11 (NIVUK)*

God's ways will be seen to be right, injustices will be addressed, wrongs righted and truth will be triumphant. Believers and nonbelievers will face Christ as Judge.

> *You, then, why do you judge your brother or sister? Or why do you treat them with contempt? For we will all stand before God's judgment seat. It is written:*
> *"'As surely as I live,' says the Lord,*

> *'every knee will bow before me;*
> *every tongue will acknowledge God.'"*
> So then, each of us will give an account of
> ourselves to God.
>
> *Romans 14:10-12 (NIVUK)*

Those who in life refused to repent and obey God will
find his abhorrence of sin not to have changed. His
holiness and justness means he cannot abide unrighteous-
ness. Warnings of the consequences of doing 'one's own
thing', as opposed to God's, will result in alienation from
his presence for two reasons.

First, as God is not in the business of coercion, the
decision they have made will be upheld. In freedom, the
disobedient have decided upon deliberate rejection of Jesus
Christ as Lord and Saviour. In love, God will not ignore
his own righteousness by overriding the exercise of free
will given to humanity.

Second, the wrath of God is not a vengeful, irrational
explosion of anger (as can be the case with humans);
rather, it flows from his love and holiness. As such, it is in
permanent revulsion against what is contrary to his holy
nature and will.

Today Christian thinking is dominated by the notion
of God as Love to such a degree that there is a tendency to
downplay his wrath. A. W. Tozer says:

> *The vague and tenuous hope that God is too*
> *kind to punish the ungodly has become a deadly*

opiate for the consciences of millions. [15]

The fact remains, God makes no compromise with sin – not now, not then – as the apostles Paul and John so starkly point out:

> *The wrath of God is being revealed from heaven against all the godlessness and wickedness of people, who suppress the truth by their wickedness … Therefore God gave them over in the sinful desires of their hearts to sexual impurity for the degrading of their bodies with one another. They exchanged the truth about God for a lie, and worshiped and served created things rather than the Creator – who is forever praised. Amen.*

> *Because of this, God gave them over to shameful lusts. Even their women exchanged natural sexual relations for unnatural ones. In the same way the men also abandoned natural relations with women and were inflamed with lust for one another. Men committed shameful acts with other men, and received in themselves the due penalty for their error.*

> *Furthermore, just as they did not think it worthwhile to retain the knowledge of God, so God gave them over to a depraved mind, so that they do what ought not to be done. They have become filled with every kind of wickedness,*

---

[15] A. W. Tozer; *The Knowledge of the Holy;* General Press (2019)

evil, greed and depravity. They are full of envy, murder, strife, deceit and malice. They are gossips, slanderers, God-haters, insolent, arrogant and boastful; they invent ways of doing evil; they disobey their parents; they have no understanding, no fidelity, no love, no mercy. Although they know God's righteous decree that those who do such things deserve death, they not only continue to do these very things but also approve of those who practice them.

Romans 1:18,24-32 (NIVUK)

Coming out of his mouth is a sharp sword with which to strike down the nations. 'He will rule them with an iron sceptre.' He treads the winepress of the fury of the wrath of God Almighty. ... Then I saw a great white throne and him who was seated on it. The earth and the heavens fled from his presence, and there was no place for them. And I saw the dead, great and small, standing before the throne, and books were opened. Another book was opened, which is the book of life. The dead were judged according to what they had done as recorded in the books. The sea gave up the dead that were in it, and death and Hades gave up the dead that were in them, and each person was judged according to what they had done. Then death and Hades were thrown into the lake of fire. The lake of fire is the second death. Anyone

> *whose name was not found written in the book*
> *of life was thrown into the lake of fire.*
>
> *Revelation 19:15;20:11-15 (NIVUK)*

By their refusal to turn from rebellion to repentance, from self-assertion to God-worship, sinners have effectively placed their signature on their own banishment order from God and consigned themselves to a living death. Jesus said:

> *'Whoever believes in the Son has eternal life, but whoever rejects the Son will not see life, for God's wrath remains on him.'*
>
> *John 3:36 (NIVUK)*

By refusing God's priceless offer of salvation, they carry the consequences and continue in sin. The God of freedom will not force them to do what they point blank refuse to do. Having refused God's priceless gift of salvation, they walk headlong into sin and, as such, God will banish them to their chosen path.[16]

For Christ's followers the story will be vastly different. That born-again transformation begun on earth will expand to limitless depths of joy, peace and praise as they enter into that perfect union with God himself – God, whose word, given in promise, is finally and completely brought to pass in perfect reality. That walk of faith, now shrouded in mystery, will clear to make all things known. High and above all else will be the sight of him, our Lord Christ, who died to bring life in all its fullness. What joy,

---

[16] See Isaiah 59:2; Luke 16:19-31; Romans 2:8

what peace, what wonder, where the faithful, called to be like him, will share finally in the fullness of his presence![17]

Alexander McLaren writes:

> *In heaven, after "ages of ages" of growing glory, we shall have to say, as each new wave of the shoreless, sunlit sea bears us onward, "It doth not yet appear what we shall be like."*[18]

That which began and blossomed in history will become imperishable fruit:

> *Then the angel showed me the river of the water of life, as clear as crystal, flowing from the throne of God and of the Lamb down the middle of the street of the city. On each side of the river stood the tree of life, bearing fruit...*
>
> *Revelation 22:1,2 (NIVUK)*

In the splendour of that new dawn where the Son reigns and where there will be no more night, those in Christ will see their Lord covered in glory! They will look into the face of him who, by his own life, saved them. At one with God, they shall enter into that perfect radiance, joy and peace. This, is life, life eternal![19]

---

[17] See 1 John 3:2;4:17; Revelation 5:6ff
[18] *Great Quotes and Illustrations;* compiled by George Sweeting; Word Books
[19] See Revelation 22:5; 1 Corinthians 13:12; Revelation 22:4

QUESTIONS

Live life God's way or our own way. What has God done for us that we can't do for ourselves? How should we live now before we die?

Today Christian thinking is dominated by God as Love; there is a tendency to downplay his wrath. What do you make of this and Paul's words in Romans 1:18,24-32 (see pp.27,28)?

Present a summary of what heaven will be like for believers.

5

Is Religion All About War?

IS THERE SUCH A THING AS A HOLY WAR? THE Arabic term *jihad* speaks of the challenge and struggle against sin and to live out the best of the Muslim faith personally and communally. However, as well as a spiritual meaning, *jihad* has a military meaning where 'holy war' can involve the use of force and destruction. The Bible's holy war is very different. It is a conflict in which we have a Holy Warrior God. He's the one who does the fighting for his people. He bids us to 'take the sword of the Spirit, which is the Word of God'[20]. Prayer and praise of God will lead us to victory!

Jehoshaphat the king of Judah made great strides forward in matters of faith and obedience to God. His international status, great building programmes and disciplined army characterised his reign. In time of war he led by valour and religious fervour. At a point when everything was going well, the nation of Judah found herself faced with the terrifying sight of a vast invading army on the horizon, baying for blood and treasure. A shaken King Jehoshaphat prayed to God[21] and ordered a nationwide fast. Next, he took his place before the assembled people of Judah and prayed publicly. We read

---

[20] Ephesians 6:17 (NLT)
[21] See 2 Chronicles 20:6-11

that 'all the men of Judah with their wives and children and little ones, stood there before the LORD'[22]. The Spirit of the Lord spoke through Jahaziel the prophet to the king and the people, saying:

> 'Do not be afraid or discouraged because of this vast army. For the battle is not yours, but God's ... You will not have to fight this battle. Take up your position; stand firm and see the deliverance the LORD will give you ... Go out and face them...'
>
> 2 Chronicles 20:15-17 (NIVUK)

The people followed the king's example; as he bowed low, so did they, with their faces to the ground.[23] Early next morning King Jehoshaphat called his people, summoning them to have faith in God and adding, 'Give thanks to the LORD, for his love endures for ever.'[24] The army set off in a chorus of praise to God.

This is quite remarkable as the battlefield is not normally a place of worship and praise! As believers, the worst and most frightening experiences, when steeped in prayer and praise to our God, will always release his mighty power, however dark the night. There is no contest between darkness and the Light of the World.

What happens next is utterly astonishing. We read that the Lord 'set ambushes' against the enemies of his people. In short, the enemy found themselves facing other enemies. In the end they slaughtered each other. When the army of

---

[22] 2 Chronicles 20:13 (NIVUK)
[23] See 2 Chronicles 20:18
[24] 2 Chronicles 20:21 (NIVUK)

Judah reached the scene, instead of a vast army they found corpses everywhere. God always wins![25]

In Britain in recent times, Brexit has caused widespread confusion and division. Most of us have never known a time like it. The European Union's unity appears to be tipping dangerously towards the edge. In our global world we live with the threat of radicals blowing themselves to pieces and taking innocent men, women and children with them. In our families we all have to deal with a range of issues concerning health, relationships and moral choices; things we did and said, best forgotten; dreams we had, shattered…

We're all left asking, where from here? As soldiers of Christ we have an enemy to face and fight. Who is the enemy? Not people, not nations, not authorities, but schemes and philosophies, systems and ideologies designed to work against humanity, devaluing and destroying. The chief enemy is Satan and his cohorts. In today's world many don't take him seriously. Satan's greatest weapon is to blind people as to his reality. The powers of darkness are a timebomb set to obliterate. But do not be afraid or discouraged; our God, as Holy Warrior, will drive Satan into oblivion. Jesus said, 'Now Satan, the ruler of this world, will be thrown out…'[26]

The thing that held centre stage with King Jehoshaphat was that he sought the Lord in prayer. When our lives are under threat, our faith is passing through dark terrain, our marriage has become shaky, the morality of our children

---

[25] See 2 Chronicles 20:22-30
[26] John 12:31 (MSG)

or ourselves is failing and we are threatened by many of Satan's devices, we must seek the Lord in fervent prayer and praise.

In our home we host a small group Bible Study. After we've concluded our sharing of God's Word, we engage in a time of prayer and praising him. Focused on the cost of faith, some followers of Christ have had to endure great trial. We draw inspiration from how bravely they took the blows.

Paul and Silas in the jail at Philippi,[27] while not having been protected by God from attack by their enemies, nonetheless escaped death. What a beating they endured though! They were clamped in irons, placed in a manhole (not in some antiseptic prison) and did not know if hanging, beheading or further flogging loomed. But what did they do? Pray and sing to God!

So when you hit the dirt and the bottom is falling out of your world, do what people would consider crazy: pray and praise God! Why? Because the vast army out there will not defeat you. God is on your side. Already he's set a trap. Ambush and crushing of the enemy is a sure thing.

We refuse to rest while the world bleeds. The open wounds of oppression and exploitation, the brutalising and bestial treatment of human beings, the shame of the starving and the horror of the lost must grab our attention. We cannot be a Christian and not be a soldier of Christ. Yes, put on the armour of God and rush to the battlefield. After all, God has already gone ahead of you.[28]

---

[27] See Acts 16
[28] See Ephesians 6:10-18; 2 Chronicles 20:1-22

The world is unprincipled. It is dog-eat-dog out there! The world doesn't fight fair. But we don't live or fight our battles that way – never have and never will. The tools of our trade aren't for marketing or manipulation, but they are for demolishing that entire massively corrupt culture. We use our powerful God-tools for smashing warped philosophies, tearing down barriers erected against the truth of God, fitting every loose thought and emotion and impulse into the structure of life shaped by Christ. Our tools are ready at hand for clearing the ground of every obstruction and building lives of obedience into maturity.

2 Corinthians 10:3-6 (MSG)

God is strong, and he wants those who follow him to be strong. So take everything the Master has set out for you, well-made weapons of the best materials. And put them to use so you will be able to stand up to everything the Devil throws your way. This is no afternoon athletic contest that we'll walk away from and forget about in a couple of hours. This is for keeps, a life-or-death fight to the finish against the Devil and all his angels. Be prepared. You are up against far more than you can handle on your own. Take all the help you can get, every weapon God has issued, so that when it's all over but the shouting you'll still be on your feet. Truth, righteousness, peace, faith, and salvation are more than words. Learn how to apply them.

You'll need them throughout your life. God's Word is an indispensable weapon. In the same way, prayer is essential in this ongoing warfare. Pray hard and long. Pray for your brothers and sisters. Keep your eyes open. Keep each other's spirits up so that no one falls behind or drops out.

Ephesians 6:10-13 (MSG)

QUESTIONS

Explain why prayer and praise to God leads to victory over the forces of evil.

Paul and Silas, faithful to God, were unjustly and severely flogged, clamped in irons and thrown into jail. Despite the pain, they prayed and woke up other prisoners with their hymn-singing! What does this say to you about their response to persecution?

The hymn, 'Onward Christian soldiers marching as to war' strongly makes the case that followers of Christ are in a war zone. Who and what is the enemy? Make a list of the practical and spiritual tools needed to win the battle.

6

Are You Lost or Found?

TODAY, IS THERE A STREET WHERE FAMILIES ARE not at war? Relationships flounder and fail, while moral standards cry for answers. The rising incidence of road rage, drug abuse, sexual promiscuity, greed and corruption rot human relations and make the world an ever more threatening and dangerous place. Most worrying of all, society in general has lost its way. Unless and until they meet with God, they remain a people lost.

What has brought about this state of affairs in the first place? It didn't start yesterday. Man is in a state of rebellion against God. His problem is perennial and internal. You find the root cause in the first book of the Bible. The 'origin' or 'beginning', otherwise called Genesis, in a real sense turned out to be the end. In chapters 2 and 3, under God, Adam and Eve had it all together so long as they listened and followed God exclusively. The moment they accepted Satan's suggestion to explore an alternative path, they found themselves partnered to the Evil One, out in the cold, abandoned, lost. Break with God's commands and you come tumbling down from that perfect oneness with God. This is often referred to as 'the fall'. That once perfect union is severed.

The fall and the forbidden 'apple' are two sides of the same coin. God had made himself perfectly clear when he said:

> *'You are free to eat from any tree in the garden;*
> *but you must not eat from the tree of*
> *knowledge of good and evil, for when you eat*
> *of it you will certainly die.'*
>
> *Genesis 2:16,17 (NIVUK)*

Instead, their decision to accept the you-will-die option of the Tempter led to catastrophic alienation from God, resulting in death.

Today the Tempter still comes in many guises, offering fame and fortune, appealing to pride, promoting independent will. '...each person is tempted,' we read in James 1:14, 'when they are dragged away by their own evil desire and enticed.'[29] On the surface, independent choice and personal pride appear reasonable, normal and therefore right. But that is precisely the problem. The 'normal' we see around us happens to be part of a fallen creation and as such is not synonymous with rightness and godliness.

These issues are scrutinised by the apostle Paul:

> *...in order that the righteous requirement of the*
> *law might be fully met in us, who do not live*
> *according to the flesh but according to the*
> *Spirit. Those who live according to the flesh*
> *have their minds set on what the flesh desires;*
> *but those who live in accordance with the Spirit*
> *have their minds set on what the Spirit desires.*
> *The mind governed by the flesh is death, but the*
> *mind governed by the Spirit is life and peace.*
> *The mind governed by the flesh is hostile to*

---

[29] NIVUK

God; it does not submit to God's law, nor can
it do so. Those who are in the realm of the flesh
cannot please God.

Romans 8:4-8 (NIVUK)

Human nature is naturally sinful; the mind is polluted
and hostile to God. The sinful body is like clockwork; in
time, the clock stops ticking, then we die. Only through
another death, that of Jesus Christ, can there be rescue and
resurrection, a way back to God, a deathblow to death and
a start of new life in all its fullness.

You see, at just the right time, when we were
still powerless, Christ died for the ungodly.
Very rarely will anyone die for a righteous
person, though for a good person someone
might possibly dare to die. But God demon-
strates his own love for us in this: while we were
still sinners, Christ died for us.

Romans 5:6-8 (NIVUK)

Today, 'multi' (meaning 'many' or 'combining') is a
key word: multicultural, multifaith, multilingual and so
on. There is an effort to dialogue, communicate and so
understand ways of life different from our own. This has
a positive side, in that it can clear the ground of prejudice
and suspicion making way for healthy and productive
relationships. (Otherwise, some thoughts and feelings can
sow seeds of discord and destruction between peoples.)
While an understanding of other faiths and cultures is to
be encouraged, there is a subtle danger that some
Christians, for the sake of 'good relations' and 'not to
offend', can find themselves in a position where to

41

proclaim the exclusivity of the gospel (where Jesus is Lord and God) is an embarrassment – but why?

In the Gospels Jesus refers to himself as 'I am' – a term used only by and for God in the Old Testament.[30] Jesus is not *a* light in the world, but *the* light and life of the world. He's not one amongst many ways, as some might imagine, that lead to God. He only is *the* road to God. To his disciples, querying about the journey of life that leads to God, he says:

> *'I am the way and the truth and the life. No one comes to the Father except through me. If you really know me, you will know my Father as well. From now on, you do know him and have seen him.'*
>
> *John 8:12; 14:6 (NIVUK)*

---

[30] See Exodus 3:13,14

QUESTIONS

What makes Christ's death on the cross different from all other deaths?

Sin is personal, perennial and destructive. How has God dealt with it and what must humans do spiritually and practically in their response to God and others?

Are you lost or found? Explain what 'lost and found' means in scriptural terms and add some examples from your own journey of faith.

7

What is Meant by God Reigning?

GOD RULES IN LOVE AND JUSTICE. EVERY FOL-
lower is accountable to him in faithfulness to his Word and
costly service to others.

God does not brook any rivals or competition. He's
number one. His people, the nations and the individual,
ignore or oppose him at their peril. Those selected for
special saving and protection carry an obligation of
faithful service to God. But it doesn't end there. It
encompasses those within their immediate circle of family,
friends and community.

> *Sing to God, sing in praise of his name,*
> *extol him who rides on the clouds;*
> *rejoice before him – his name is the Lord.*
> *A father to the fatherless, a defender of widows,*
> *is God in his holy dwelling.*
> *God sets the lonely in families,*
> *he leads out the prisoners with singing;*
> *but the rebellious live in a sun-scorched land.*
> *When you, God, went out before your people,*
> *when you marched through the wilderness*
> ...
> *Your people settled in it,*
> *and from your bounty, God, you provided*
> *for the poor.*

> *The Lord announces the word,*
>   *and the women who proclaim it are a mighty*
>   *throng...*

Psalm 68:4-7,10-11 (NIVUK)

God's victory parade here evokes great bursts of cheer and worship. He is the 'father to the fatherless, a defender of widows'; reaching the homeless and freeing the imprisoned is what God is about. His people are compelled to do likewise.

> *This is what the LORD says:*
>   *'What fault did your ancestors find in me,*
>   *that they strayed so far from me?*
>   *They followed worthless idols*
>   *and became worthless themselves.*
>
>   *...*
>
>   *I brought you into a fertile land*
>   *to eat its fruit and rich produce.*
>   *But you came and defiled my land*
>   *and made my inheritance detestable.*
>
>   *...*
>
>   *Cross over to the coasts of Cyprus and look,*
>   *send to Kedar and observe closely;*
>   *see if there has ever been anything like this:*
>   *has a nation ever changed its gods?*
>   *(Yet they are not gods at all.)*
>   *But my people have exchanged their glorious God*
>   *for worthless idols.*
>   *Be appalled at this, you heavens,*
>   *and shudder with great horror,'*

> *declares the* LORD.
>
> *Jeremiah 2:5,7,10-12 (NIVUK)*

The prophet Jeremiah is not into speaking 'sweet nothings'. He shoots his arrow straight to the heart. Those who were rescued by God from slavery into glorious freedom are now on a charge of desertion from the conquering God. They have traded God for false gods and are plunged into a cesspool of slavery more sinister than their forefathers endured under the brutality of the pharaohs of Egypt!

Today's culture in the Western world is no different. Some are crazed with self. Church buildings are emptying at a shocking speed. Materialism and secularism are stealing a race on religion. Faith in God has declined alarmingly. Faith in 'me' has rocketed. More and more people are chasing dreams of money, fame and power. These are today's gods.

After faith, family is the most important unit in society, but the levels of immorality, violence and abuse are sowing the seeds of its destruction. God who reigns also judges. The verdict is given: guilty! Only he can turn the tide and save his people.

Often we expect to be rewarded or receive some recognition for things we do. How often do we 'spend ourselves' exploring and finding ways of 'doing good' to those who cannot, or indeed *will* not, give us anything in return? In Luke's Gospel, Jesus and others shared a meal at the table of a leading Pharisee. All eyes were on Jesus. After healing a man with hugely swollen joints he told a story, one that hit out at those who craved the attention and adoration of others.

'When someone invites you to a wedding feast, do not take the place of honour, for a person more distinguished than you may have been invited. If so, the host who invited both of you will come and say to you, "Give this person your seat." Then, humiliated, you will have to take the least important place. But when you are invited, take the lowest place, so that when your host comes, he will say to you, "Friend, move up to a better place." Then you will be honoured in the presence of all the other guests. For all those who exalt themselves will be humbled, and those who humble themselves will be exalted.'

Luke 14:8-11 (NIVUK)

Pride, power and prestige defined the Pharisees. They knew nothing of humility and always wanted a front seat. Give it time, though, and they'd tumble from their perch, as the host described by Jesus brought forward to first place the one contented to take a back seat!

Pope Francis has to be the kind of person Jesus had in mind: a man who's uncomfortable with the posh trimmings of high office. When archbishop in Argentine before his election to the Papacy, he loved spending time amongst the poor of Argentine. Rather than travel by the church's limo, he took the bus! That same low profile remains. The exotic splendour of the Vatican cuts no ice with this man who lives in the Vatican Guesthouse, not the Papal Apartments.

Today, God invites us to receive and share in the delights of his love and generosity. We come as we are. We leave behind all ambition to promote ourselves at another's expense. Above all, he calls us to go in search of those not normally part of our inner circle of friends and family. At first, our outreach efforts may take a bit of getting used to, perhaps even be uncomfortable. But if Christ lives in us, then the Holy Spirit will teach and guide us wherever we go, whatever we do in his name.

Let the people come with their broken bodies and messed minds, their rough, rugged ways, course talk and rude gestures. Let them come with their wealth and pride. God loves them as much as he loves us! He invites them to his table where appetite for Jesus, the Bread of Life is a winner ticket. Need and greed sit together and feed on the King's menu. Prepare to win them for Christ and give to each pride of place!

God's love in action

Our God, who is number one and who calls us to be faithful, also requires that we learn to reach out to others by living and practising his precious love between ourselves. God's love in action begins in us, between us and through us to the needy in society.

> *Keep on loving one another as brothers and sisters. Do not forget to show hospitality to strangers, for by so doing some people have shown hospitality to angels without knowing it. Continue to remember those in prison as if you were together with them in prison, and those who are ill-treated as if you yourselves were suffering. ... Through Jesus, therefore, let us*

continually offer to God a sacrifice of praise –
the fruit of lips that openly profess his name.
And do not forget to do good and to share with
others, for with such sacrifices God is pleased.

Hebrews 13:1-3,15-16 (NIVUK)

In this Bible passage the apostle takes love as pure and godly. The one who loves feels into the pain and plight of others – people they don't know; people fallen on hard times, desperate for a bed, a meal, some understanding; people behind prison bars and those subjected to the tyranny of abuse; people manacled to money. All need help. If only believers knew, some are even angels in disguise as Abraham experienced![31]

Marriage should be honoured by all, and the
marriage bed kept pure, for God will judge the
adulterer and all the sexually immoral.

Hebrews 13:4 (NIVUK)

God of the needy also reigns over marriage. It is a covenant before God between husband and wife. They, though distinct, have become 'one flesh'[32]. The term is an attempt to define just how much they each belong to each other under God's hand. Sex itself between them is a sacred act. Outside this state it is not.

Pause

I invite you to reach for the Bible and take time to read, listen and follow the message God wants you to hear on

---

[31] See Genesis 18:1-33
[32] Ephesians 5:31 (NIVUK)

the journey of faith. Take a look at Genesis 2:22-24, Proverbs 30:18-19, Ephesians 5:22-33 and Matthew 19:4-6.

In today's world, even amongst some believers, we are witnessing God's clear and firm line on marriage being replaced by same-sex marriages. Scripture is not open to discussion on this matter. God's people who scrap or bend his commands to accommodate their own fancies will face the judgement of he who reigns!

The love and lust for money (materialism) is another god of this age.[33] God's people must be masters, not slaves, of possessions. Contentment with the simple pleasures of life where God reigns is primary.

Church leaders must be Christ-like models who share the Word of God faithfully. As such we value them and trust their leadership.

Yes, our God is first in all things. He holds us accountable for how we live. He invites us to come to his table of plenty in humility. He calls us each to live and love like Christ!

Here are some further passages from God's Word on the subject of marriage and family, which I encourage you to study: 1 Corinthians 7:1-16; Colossians 3:18-19; Hebrews 13:4-7 and Mark 10:6-9.

---

[33] See 1 Timothy 6:10

QUESTIONS

God rules in love and justice. He brooks no rivals. He's boss. Where people's thoughts, words and actions disregard his will, He holds them to account. Give some examples of God's way and our way.

Materialism, secularism, pride and power have ambushed the lives of many today. What does the believer need to know, be, say and do as a witness of God?

What does the Bible say about marriage? How important is it to do as God says?

8

What is the Kingdom of God?

IN THE BIBLE, 'ETERNAL LIFE' IS SYNONYMOUS with 'life in the kingdom of God'. The word 'kingdom' denotes that others are included. This is no private matter; say 'kingdom' and you say 'community'. Only those transformed by the hand of God belong as citizens of his kingdom. Such a life is shared, precious and unique precisely because it springs out of perfect communion with God. The apostle John writes:

> *The infinite Life of God himself took shape before us. We saw it, we heard it, and now we're telling you so you can experience it along with us, this experience of communion with the Father and his Son, Jesus Christ. Our motive for writing is simply this: We want you to enjoy this, too. Your joy will double our joy!*
>
> *1 John 1:2-4 (MSG)*

History confirms that Church schemes to establish the kingdom in this world are futile. The naive optimism that gripped the 19th century was soon exploded by the 'war to end all wars'[34] followed by the Second World War and the hundreds of conflicts, bloody revolutions and acts of terrorism ever since; these bear testimony to the fact that

---

[34] i.e. the First World War

even the best of people lack the power to bring about God's kingdom on earth.

Film director Steven Spielberg in *Schindler's List* and *Saving Private Ryan* recreates haunting images of war. More recently there have been accounts of atrocities and bombings in Manchester, London, Berlin and Brussels, as well as in France, Denmark, Norway and many other countries. All this demonstrates that humankind frequently fails even to deliver justice, equity and peace, let alone establish God's kingdom.

Man's ideas are different from God's. It is God and God alone who creates the kingdom. What he does stands forever. Man's knowhow cannot create it nor his folly frustrate it. When Jesus prays, 'Your kingdom come,'[35] this is not a plea for utopia here and now. Jesus is not suggesting the kingdom will be brought about by human agencies or powers. These words relate rather to what God will do through his Son when he returns to earth and, ultimately, when this universe no longer exists.

With the words, 'The Lord is coming soon!'[36] Paul mirrors the longing of the early church. Only at Christ's second coming at the end of the age will the full impact of the kingdom be known.

The Church has much to learn from those first believers who very much lived in the atmosphere of the end time. With intense urgency they spread the gospel and clung to the promise given by their risen and ascended Lord – 'I'm on my way! I'll be there soon!' – to which we,

---

[35] Matthew 6:10 (NIVUK)
[36] 1 Corinthians 16:22 (NLV)

like they, respond, 'Yes! Come, Master Jesus!'[37] Does this mean we do nothing while we wait for his coming? Nothing could be farther from the truth. In fact, the complete opposite: God, through his people, is working out his eternal purposes. The kingdom values of Jesus' Sermon on the Mount[38] are to be followed by its citizens – each day as it comes.

The future is with God. The present is with us. We do not hold the blueprints of the kingdom. That is God's business. But as servants we have been given clear goals:

> *So, my dear brothers, since future victory is sure, be strong and steady, always abounding in the Lord's work, for you know that nothing you do for the Lord is ever wasted as it would be if there were no resurrection.*

1 Corinthians 15:58 (TLB)

The kingdom has implications for life now and after death. Our forebears were all too aware of this. Many Weslyans, Baptists, Brethren and Salvationists lived on the edge of eternity, believing emphatically in sin's destructive power and damnation and that only Christ could save from hell. God and the winning of souls meant everything to them. There was a gripping sense of urgency about eternal matters. Have we lost this today?

Passionate and persuasive in the practice and preaching of the gospel, matters of the 'now' were indissolubly linked to life after death. Decisions made in this life determine the joys of heaven or the terrors of hell. 'The mission of the

---

[37] Revelation 22:20 (MSG)
[38] See Matthew 5:5-7

[Salvation] Army,' said William Booth (its founder), 'is to save men; not nearly to civilise them … to save them from sin and Hell, to bring them to God and bring God to them.'

What made our forefathers special was their fearless courage. They cared nothing of public image. They shunned personal interests and placed above everything else the living and telling of the glorious gospel. The cost did not count. Speaking as a Salvationist, I'm happy to repeat what others have said: 'We are an Army without guns.' We are not spiritual pacifists. Spiritual warfare is our business. Either we engage the enemy or we die. We have no peace accord with evil or its master. With evangelistic fervour and holy aggression, we take our stand against sin, injustice, oppression and exploitation. These are our battlefronts.

Recently my wife and I attended the reunion celebration of fellow students in ministry after fifty years since our ordination and commissioning as Salvation Army Officers. The event was led by retired Territorial Commander of the United Kingdom, Commissioner Alex Hughes. While in high office I remember a public meeting where he called on Salvationists to be 'people of passion, full of fire: the fire of the Holy Spirit'.

There is no other way forward in the journey for all of God's people than to be on fire for God. This fire, this power of the Holy Spirit, will ultimately enable and empower the believer to be what those earlier believers were: living in the atmosphere of the 'end time', urgently grasping every opportunity by life and word and deed to reach the world with the message of the gospel…

Another fire, hell's fire, 'never goes out'[39]. Those who suffer its agony do so without end.

---

[39] Mark 9:44 (NIVUK)

QUESTIONS

What do you think the kingdom of God has to do with perfect communion with God?

Can human effort lead to a realisation of God's kingdom on earth? If so, how? If not, why?

What are the implications of the kingdom of God here and now?

In the Lord's Prayer we say, 'Your kingdom come, your will be done…' After reading Mark 13, comment on: What are the signs of Christ's coming? Who knows when it will happen? How crucial is it that we should be alert and on our guard?

9

What is it Like to Walk With God?

IN THE OLD TESTAMENT, PSALM 121 IS ONE OF the pilgrim psalms. It traces the journey of life and faith and celebrates the fact that God's guardian care provides strength and protection from any and every calamity life can throw at you.

> *I lift up my eyes to the mountains –*
>   *where does my help come from?*
> *My help comes from the LORD,*
>   *the Maker of heaven and earth.*
>
> *Psalm 121:1-2 (NIVUK)*

Don't be sentimental about this; the hills then were where bankrupt versions of faith took place. Often they were venues of idolatrous practices, frightening shrines and elaborate altars to pagan gods, especially the worship of Baal. In Jeremiah we read:

> *For they have forsaken me and made this a place of foreign gods; they have burned incense in it to gods that neither they nor their ancestors nor the kings of Judah ever knew, and they have filled this place with the blood of the innocent. They have built the high places of Baal to burn their children in the fire as offerings to Baal –*

> *something I did not command or mention, nor
> did it enter my mind.*
>
> *Jeremiah 19:4-5 (NIVUK)*

In our world today, a pagan and heathen way of life has become the norm for many. It may be listed under the banner of 'freedom of choice' but it enslaves and robs people of liberty and life that only God can give.

The mountains, though inspiring to look at, fail to be the source of saving and preservation of God's people. The late Rev. George Duncan points out that in this psalm the psalmist realised: how small he felt in the sight of God; how safe he felt in the hands of God; and how sure he felt of the help of God.[40]

David could never have sung, 'I go to the hills, for the sound of music!' No way. Instead, he says, '...where does my help come from? My help comes from the LORD, the Maker of heaven and earth'[41] (not from the hills).

> *By faith – by believing God – we know that the
> world and the stars – in fact, all things – were
> made at God's command; and that they were all
> made from things that can't be seen.*
>
> *Hebrews 11:3 (TLB)*

None of us know what tomorrow will bring, but where faith is placed in God, one can say with trust:

> *I'm in His hands,
> whate'er the future holds,*

---

[40] Rev. George Duncan; *Preach the Word;* Marshall, Morgan and Scott
[41] Psalm 121:1-2 (NIVUK)

> *I'm in his hands;*
> *The days I cannot see*
>   *have all been planned for me;*
> *His way is best, you see,*
>   *I'm in His hands.*[42]

The journey to Zion and the Holy City of Jerusalem, for King David and all who made it, was a pilgrimage. In Hebrew history pilgrims journeyed to Shiloh, Dan and Bethel. The ultimate destination was Jerusalem. There were valleys to be crossed; mountains to be climbed; bogs to plough through; wild animals, in some cases, to be faced! The perils of the journey were not known in advance but security in God was a sure thing. The Psalmist was on the ball when he said, 'Those who look to him [God] are radiant; their faces are never covered with shame.'[43]

How well I remember the beautiful tenor voice of Mario Lanza. The song that thrilled me as a young Christian was *I'll Walk With God.* In journeying with God, there's a leaning on him by those who follow, and a deep trust and security. However trying life gets, faith exercised eradicates fear where the walker's hand has firmly clasped God's.

I turn to the words of the late General Albert Orsborn of The Salvation Army who, following a great tragedy in his life, visited the 'hot healing springs' in New Zealand. There he captured the essence of journeying with God when he wrote:

---

[42] Stanley E. Ditmer (1924-2003); 'I'm in his hands'
[43] Psalm 34:5 (NIVUK)

Life is a journey, long is the road
And when the noontide is high
Souls that are weary faint 'neath the load,
Long for the waters and cry:
The well is deep and I require
A draught of the water of life...
Life is a seeking, life is a quest
Eager and longing desire
Unto the true things, unto the best,
Godward our spirits aspire...
Life is a finding; vain wanderings cease
When from the Saviour we claim
All we have longed for, solace and peace,
And we have life in his name.

We used to sing in our church, 'Not weary yet...' That's great but often in life we do experience our 'down days'. These are the times when we can easily put a foot wrong and stumble. The Hebrew word defines it as 'slip, slide, stagger'.

One Valentine's Day I took my wife Helen up the Clyde Valley, not far from where we now live in central Scotland. The sky was blue, the sun shone brightly. We pulled into a garden centre and shared a lovely lunch in the new upgraded restaurant there. The place was crowded and full of elderly people of which we, of course, were the only 'recycled teenagers'!

'Darling,' I said to Helen, 'how sad that so many are dependent on walking sticks.' More than once I was ready to spring to my feet to help those unsteady on their feet. Glad to say, no one fell while we were there.

In the days of weariness that cause us to stagger, sway and slip, those are the times to turn our weariness on its head and be 'watchful'.

> *The LORD preserves those who are true to him,*
> *but the proud he pays back in full. Be strong*
> *and take heart, all you who hope in the Lord.*
> *Psalm 31:23,24 (NIVUK).*

I love to hear our brass band play a piece entitled *His Guardian Care*. The images projected on screen add to the richness of its message and appeal. When God spoke with his people in bondage to Egyptian slavery, he made a promise that in time was realised:

> *'Therefore, say to the Israelites: "I am the*
> *LORD, and I will bring you out from under the*
> *yoke of the Egyptians. I will free you from being*
> *slaves to them, and I will redeem you with an*
> *outstretched arm and with mighty acts of*
> *judgment. I will take you as my own people,*
> *and I will be your God. Then you will know*
> *that I am the LORD your God, who brought you*
> *out from under the yoke of the Egyptians."'*
> *Exodus 6:6-7 (NIVUK)*

As a young man I worked as a labourer for a time in a printer's factory. I used to have to take my turn on the night shift. On one occasion I was trying to move a large trolley where wastepaper was stored. It had high sides and I was puzzled by how difficult it was to move it forward. I stopped and peered into the load only to find a well-rounded young man spread-eagled and sound asleep. I made the appropriate noises and he jumped into the air like a jack-in-the-box, red-faced and very embarrassed.

You'll never find God sleeping on the job! Were our God to take a nap, how worried we'd be. Imagine what disasters would hit our world while he was 'out of it'.

North Korea keeps hitting the headlines – and it is hardly surprising… but we can rest easy in the knowledge that our God neither slumbers nor sleeps[44] – no turning his face away, no distraction, no detachment. Our God is ever 'on the job'. He is a sure source of strength and security. He stands right at your side through all the challenges and changes of life.

Whatever threats, real or imagined, God holds, protects and preserves you! He says:

> *I have put my words in your mouth and covered you with the shadow of my hand – I who set the heavens in place, who laid the foundations of the earth, and who say to Zion, 'You are my people.'*
>
> *Isaiah 51:16 (NIVUK)*

He is your shield and shade from the blast of the elements and evil.

> *You have been a refuge for the poor, a refuge for the needy in their distress, a shelter from the storm and a shade from the heat. For the breath*

---

[44] See Psalm 121:4

> *of the ruthless is like a storm driving against a wall.*
>
> *Isaiah 25:4 (NIVUK)*

Hear Jesus' prayer before his execution:

> *'I will remain in the world no longer, but they are still in the world, and I am coming to you. Holy Father, protect them by the power of your name, the name you gave me, so that they may be one as we are one.'*
>
> *John 17:11 (NIVUK)*

The apostle Paul, writing to Timothy, speaks graphically of his sufferings for Christ, urging the young man to endure, to be faithful and to live and preach the Word of God. He then adds:

> *But the Lord stood at my side and gave me strength, so that through me the message might be fully proclaimed and all the Gentiles might hear it. And I was delivered from the lion's mouth. The Lord will rescue me from every evil attack and will bring me safely to his heavenly kingdom.*
>
> *2 Timothy 4:17-18 (NIVUK)*

Whatever happens to me, to you, to yours, to our world in the future, know that God is our shield and defender. Let's shout it from the rooftops:

> *My help comes from the LORD, the Maker of heaven and earth!*
>
> *Psalm 121:2 (NIVUK)*

QUESTIONS

In our journey with God what challenges are we likely to face and what resources should we draw upon?

Explain, as to an unbeliever, what it is in the life of the Christian that gives reason for celebration, comfort, healing and hope.

Jesus prays God's protection on his followers and Paul testifies to rescue from the lion's mouth. What is it like in your life as a believer to walk with God?

10

What Matters Most in Life? (1)

'I'M TELLING YOU, JIM, ONCE AND FOR ALL!' AS A child I often gave my mother cause to bellow a stern warning to bring this stubborn, strong-headed 'know it all' lad into line. The generation gap's always there; old and new do not always sit comfortably together.

As a Salvation Army Officer in retirement, I enjoy the privilege to serve part-time as a chaplain for the NHS near Glasgow, Scotland. You can't miss the poster around the hospital that says, 'What matters to you?'

The Bible, though ancient, speaks of what matters most in life loud and clear. Join me in taking a good look at this.

Love God and Others

For many, life is about meeting *my* wants. Personal satisfaction becomes all-consuming. Deuteronomy 6:1-9 is the foundational building block of human survival and the quality of life. It begins with listening to God and learning how to reach out to others.

> *These are the commands, decrees and laws the LORD your God directed me to teach you to observe in the land that you are crossing the Jordan to possess, so that you, your children and their children after them may fear the LORD your God as long as you live by keeping all his*

*decrees and commands that I give you, and so
that you may enjoy long life. Hear, Israel, and
be careful to obey so that it may go well with
you and that you may increase greatly in a land
flowing with milk and honey, just as the LORD,
the God of your ancestors, promised you. Hear,
O Israel: the LORD our God, the LORD is one.
Love the LORD your God with all your heart
and with all your soul and with all your
strength. These commandments that I give you
today are to be on your hearts. Impress them on
your children. Talk about them when you sit at
home and when you walk along the road, when
you lie down and when you get up. Tie them as
symbols on your hands and bind them on your
foreheads. Write them on the door-frames of
your houses and on your gates.*

Deuteronomy 6:1-9 (NIVUK)

There is only *one* God. 'Hear, O Israel: the LORD our
God, the LORD is one.'[45] This clarion call to 'pay attention'
is otherwise known in Hebrew as the *shema*. We are to
love him with every fibre of our being.

Then in Mark's Gospel, Jesus heads up a debate with
the Jewish authorities on what was the most important
commandment.[46] He supports the *shema* and adds, 'Love
your neighbour as yourself.'[47]

---

[45] Deuteronomy 6:4 (NIVUK)
[46] Mark 12:28-34
[47] Mark 12:31 (NIVUK)

> *One of the teachers of the law came and heard*
> *them debating. Noticing that Jesus had given*
> *them a good answer, he asked him, 'Of all the*
> *commandments, which is the most important?'*
> *'The most important one,' answered Jesus, 'is*
> *this: "Hear, O Israel: the Lord our God, the*
> *Lord is one. Love the Lord your God with all*
> *your heart and with all your soul and with all*
> *your mind and with all your strength." The*
> *second is this: "Love your neighbour as your-*
> *self." There is no commandment greater than*
> *these.'*
>
> Mark 12:28-31 (NIVUK)

How then can we fail if we are fired by passion for God, steeped in prayer and energised by the Holy Spirit? Can you think of anything else that matters more in life?

Shattered – The Shadow of the Past

In Hebrews 7:23-28, the writer declares the short-comings of Jewish high priests and the traditional sacrificial system. They came, they went. The animal sacrifice for sins never hit the target. The old way fell short. Missing was the perfect High Priest. In Jesus we have that: one who not only made the sacrifice but was himself the perfect sacrifice to atone for sin. God's perfect Son does the perfect job, a one-off, a 'once for all'[48].

> *Now there have been many of those priests,*
> *since death prevented them from continuing in*

---

[48] Hebrews 7:27 (NIVUK)

> *office; but because Jesus lives for ever, he has a permanent priesthood. Therefore he is able to save completely those who come to God through him, because he always lives to intercede for them. Such a high priest truly meets our need – one who is holy, blameless, pure, set apart from sinners, exalted above the heavens. Unlike the other high priests, he does not need to offer sacrifices day after day, first for his own sins, and then for the sins of the people. He sacrificed for their sins once for all when he offered himself. For the law appoints as high priests men in all their weakness; but the oath, which came after the law, appointed the Son, who has been made perfect for ever.*
>
> *Hebrews 7:23-28 (NIVUK)*

It's often so hard to give up habits of a lifetime. Traditions, rituals and customs can, and do, have their place. The danger lies in being blinded and bound by 'the way we've always done things' and doing so in a mechanical manner where what we do impoverishes rather than enriches our lives. Change can be risky, but it can also be liberating. Supremely in life, we need to be open to new ways that carry promise of something better.

The Ultimate Sacrifice

In the case of Christ, the new way is not only the better way, it is the *only* way! It bypasses those 'dead-end efforts' to improve our spiritual fitness and faith. Christ, by the shedding of his life-blood, delivers God's master stroke to save us from ourselves. He does this by drawing us into himself and ultimately into heaven and home.

> *But when Christ came as high priest of the good things that are now already here, he went through the greater and more perfect tabernacle that is not made with human hands, that is to say, is not a part of this creation. He did not enter by means of the blood of goats and calves; but he entered the Most Holy Place once for all by his own blood, so obtaining eternal redemption. The blood of goats and bulls and the ashes of a heifer sprinkled on those who are ceremonially unclean sanctify them so that they are outwardly clean. How much more, then, will the blood of Christ, who through the eternal Spirit offered himself unblemished to God, cleanse our consciences from acts that lead to death, so that we may serve the living God!*
>
> *Hebrews 9:11-14 (NIVUK)*

Nothing is more wonderful, or matters more, than the knowledge, stamped by personal experience to give testimony, that Christ has saved us from the destructive power of sin!

The Saving that Lasts

Christ alone is able to save. His work is 'once for all'. In other aspects of life we can never say that. In industry and science, there inevitably is constant change; that's OK if it leads to life with better quality and progress. Even so, the best of human disciplines fail at the starting post. Humanity's DNA has a default to sin. King David said it:

> *I was born a sinner – yes, from the moment my mother conceived me.*
>
> *Psalm 51:5 (EXB)*

Apostle Paul put it this way:

> *...all people ... are under the power of sin.*
>
> *Romans 3:9 (NLT)*

It wrecks relationships, is guilty of all forms of abuse, and breeds violence, crime and suffering. Tragically, people generally don't take sin seriously. This is one of Satan's success stories. He blinds the minds of people to the reality and consequences of sin. The truth is, man is better at harnessing the atom than conquering himself. As General of the US Army, Omar Nelson Bradley described it, 'nuclear giants, but ethical infants'.

Some claim the Church is for a bygone age; something old-fashioned. So, too, is the air we breathe. Without it we'd not be around. Truth does not belong to the calendar. It is timeless. 'I am the way and the truth and the life,'[49] said Jesus. He alone is the only hope of the world. He alone brings saving that lasts. Is there another way? *No!* My mother never settled the matter – God did. Once for all, for time and eternity, to the nations of the world, to you and to me, the broken and the lost, Christ is *the* answer!

---

[49] John 14:6 (NIVUK)

QUESTIONS

What makes God's commands and saving power utterly unique and crucial to life and eternal survival?

Explain what sin is and provide some examples that explain how God has dealt with it.

Jesus said, 'I am the way and the truth and the life.' (John 14:6, NIVUK) What does this say about Jesus and his message to the world?

11

What Matters Most in Life? (2)

BESIDES THE BASIC KIT FOR SURVIVAL IN LIFE such as food, shelter, health and happiness, making the most of life equates with fame and fortune for some, while for others it has to do with holding on tight to everything and anything that feeds the appetite for satisfaction. The question is: do our feelings, our image and our physical needs being met provide the best life has to offer?

Even the word 'life' conjures up in the mind a vast array of definitions: from animal, vegetable, mineral, to how you categorise human life as distinct from every other life form. And as if this were not enough, some, like myself, who testify to seeing beyond the immediate scientific and physical universe to the person we call God, introduce into the search one who is unreachable by any mathematical equation, scientific or indeed mystical investigation. How then, given our curiosity is aroused and expanded by the depth of our search, can we arrive at a place at which God can be known?

For some, the very mention of God, never mind knowing God, is quite enough for one day, thank you, and at this juncture the 'switch off' button is pressed. But wait! Hear me further and consider these options. If you choose to climb onboard and give it a try, what have you to lose? Alternatively, blow a 'time up' whistle and you might never know what you're missing. Either way, whether you leave or remain on the journey, I suggest that a leap into the unknown could well result in an awesome reality of staggering dimensions. At the end of the day, the decision is yours.

Failure Versus Faith

In you, LORD my God,
I put my trust.
I trust in you;
do not let me be put to shame,
nor let my enemies triumph over me.
No one who hopes in you
will ever be put to shame,
but shame will come on those
who are treacherous without cause.
Show me your ways, LORD,
teach me your paths.
Guide me in your truth and teach me,
for you are God my Saviour,
and my hope is in you all day long.
Remember, LORD, your great mercy and love,
for they are from of old.
Do not remember the sins of my youth
and my rebellious ways;
according to your love remember me,
for you, LORD, are good.
Good and upright is the LORD;
therefore he instructs sinners in his ways.
He guides the humble in what is right
and teaches them his way.

Psalm 25:1-9 (NIVUK)

In life things can get hairy sometimes. For a time, we do well; then, *bang!* Dizzy, bruised and confused, we wonder, why? Like King David, we call to mind the things we said and did that make us ashamed. Where we brought this to God, he forgave. But the question is, can we forgive ourselves? Are we capable of dealing with the things that trouble, even haunt us? The truth is, some can't. David couldn't but he learned to throw in his lot with God. He got into the classroom of God's instructions. He held on tight to the hand of his Saviour, God. He opened himself up to be led step by step. Let's follow our God where he leads. He alone does for us what we cannot do for ourselves.

Deliverance Versus Death

My now teenage granddaughter, Leah, when she was a three-year-old, stamped her feet shouting, 'It's not fair, Papa! It's not fair!' Her papa told her tenderly, 'Darling, one day you'll learn that life is not fair.'

> *The word of the LORD came to me: 'What do you people mean by quoting this proverb about the land of Israel:*
> *"The parents eat sour grapes,*
> *and the children's teeth are set on edge"?*
> *As surely as I live, declares the Sovereign LORD, you will no longer quote this proverb in Israel. For everyone belongs to me, the parent as well as the child – both alike belong to me. The one who sins is the one who will die.'*
>
> ...

'Yet you say, "The way of the LORD is not just." Hear, you Israelites: is my way unjust? Is it not your ways that are unjust? If a righteous person turns from their righteousness and commits sin, they will die for it; because of the sin they have committed they will die. But if a wicked person turns away from the wickedness they have committed and does what is just and right, they will save their life. Because they consider all the offences they have committed and turn away from them, that person will surely live; they will not die. Yet the Israelites say, "The way of the LORD is not just." Are my ways unjust, people of Israel? Is it not your ways that are unjust?

'Therefore, you Israelites, I will judge each of you according to your own ways, declares the Sovereign LORD. Repent! Turn away from all your offences; then sin will not be your downfall. Rid yourselves of all the offences you have committed, and get a new heart and a new spirit. Why will you die, people of Israel? For I take no pleasure in the death of anyone, declares the Sovereign LORD. Repent and live!'

Ezekiel 18:1-4,25-32

Ancient Israel launched into a tirade of complaints against God, saying that he had dealt an indiscriminate blow against families where even the children weren't spared. In actual fact, the parents, not God, were to blame for the suffering of their children. They failed to set a good example. Little wonder the children went off the rails.

Both young and old are judged equally: do it God's way, you live; do it your own way, you die! Blunt stuff. What does God's way entail? Simply to 'own up' to failure by turning away from the big 'me' factor which fights and feeds on personal ego. Such a lifestyle, where God doesn't figure, is heading for personal and communal disaster, even death.

So far, how are you reacting to these issues? You can shrug them off as crazy – or, is your curiosity aroused so that you'd like to explore further? Is it touching a sore point where you're carrying a sense of guilt? It doesn't have to be that way. God alone is able to save from ruin. He gives a new heart! A new Spirit! He is more than fair.

Performance Versus Promise

Have you ever met people who say one thing and do another? A promise is pointless if not worked out in practice. Consider the story Jesus told in which a father asked his two sons to work his land.

> *'What do you think? There was a man who had two sons. He went to the first and said, "Son, go and work today in the vineyard." "I will not," he answered, but later he changed his mind and went. Then the father went to the other son and said the same thing. He answered, "I will, sir," but he did not go.*
>
> *'Which of the two did what his father wanted?'*

'The first,' they answered.

Jesus said to them, 'Truly I tell you, the tax collectors and the prostitutes are entering the kingdom of God ahead of you. For John came to you to show you the way of righteousness, and you did not believe him, but the tax collectors and the prostitutes did. And even after you saw this, you did not repent and believe him.'

Matthew 21:28-32

One son said no but did it; the other said yes and didn't. This illustrates 'actions speak louder than words'. Being focused and faithful to God, however hard it gets, is what counts. Many leaders of the faith in Jesus' day said yes but practised no. A reckless rage must have possessed them when Jesus told them that 'crooks and whores' who believe would be streets ahead of them in the kingdom of God! What about church members and leadership today? Some are not what they seem. Sometimes we have that chip on our shoulders or even turn up our noses at those who look and act in a manner that rattles us. Let's rather follow Jesus' example of reaching out to all in God's name.

Slave Versus Status

A lady told me recently that she's in love with Jesus. She dreams about him. Often in her dream she runs to him like a little girl and he sweeps her off her feet, into his arms. At other times she imagines herself dancing with him in sweet romance. My mind turned to Songs of Songs in scripture where intimacy features prominently not only between man and woman, but in God's bridegroom love for his people and the believer's love for his/her Lord.

> *Therefore if you have any encouragement from being united with Christ, if any comfort from his love, if any common sharing in the Spirit, if any tenderness and compassion, then make my joy complete by being like-minded, having the same love, being one in spirit and of one mind. Do nothing out of selfish ambition or vain conceit. Rather, in humility value others above yourselves, not looking to your own interests but each of you to the interests of the others. In your relationships with one another, have the same mindset as Christ Jesus:*
>
>> *who, being in very nature God,*
>> *did not consider equality with God something to be used to his own advantage;*
>> *rather, he made himself nothing*
>>> *by taking the very nature of a servant,*
>>> *being made in human likeness.*
>> *And being found in appearance as a man,*
>>> *he humbled himself*
>>> *by becoming obedient to death –*
>>>> *even death on a cross!*
>> *Therefore God exalted him to the highest place*
>>> *and gave him the name that is above every name,*
>> *that at the name of Jesus every knee should bow,*
>>> *in heaven and on earth and under the earth,*

> *and every tongue acknowledge that Jesus Christ*
> *is Lord,*
>> *to the glory of God the Father.*
> *Therefore, my dear friends, as you have always*
> *obeyed – not only in my presence, but now*
> *much more in my absence – continue to work*
> *out your salvation with fear and trembling, for*
> *it is God who works in you to will and to act in*
> *order to fulfil his good purpose.*
>
> *Philippians 2:1-13*

This passage expresses the unique relationship Jesus had with his Father God – something the people of God are invited to share in. As we do, there are big lessons to be learned.

Ambrose, one of the 'greats' of the early church, cared deeply for people. When the local bishop died, discussions focused on his successor. A child's voice arose: 'Ambrose – bishop!' The gathering joined in. Ambrose would have none of it. He went into hiding. Later the Emperor persuaded Ambrose to accept and he became Bishop of Milan. Humility defined this man. The lessons are plain. Deal with vanity and pride. Be content to take a backseat. Resist doing things to get noticed. Be ready to congratulate and cooperate with those entrusted with special responsibility over you. They are not better than you but are worthy of respect.

The apostle Paul appeals for humility and service that takes its lead example from Jesus himself. He writes:

> *Think of yourselves the way Christ Jesus*
> *thought of himself. He had equal status with*

God but didn't think so much of himself that he
had to cling to the advantages of that status no
matter what. Not at all. When the time came,
he set aside the privileges of deity and took on
the status of a slave, became human! Having
become human, he stayed human. It was an
incredibly humbling process. He didn't claim
special privileges. Instead, he lived a selfless,
obedient life and then died a selfless, obedient
death – and the worst kind of death at that – a
crucifixion.

Philippians 2:5-11 (MSG)

Paul presents us here with a sketch of the unique nature of Jesus. He has status and – no mistake – he is God! Yet he gives up that privileged position to become a human! Slave versus status? Christ Jesus claimed no special status. Instead, he lived entirely for God and others. Utterly obedient to his Father God, he gave himself to the worst kind of death: crucifixion. For this God honoured and exalted him above all.

What contribution are we making to the body of Christ and the community where we live? Are there things in our thinking and behaviour which get in the way of being like Christ? What matters is that we, by God's grace become more and more like Jesus: love him; live for him; be like him. This is impossible on our own but a sure reality when energised by God the Holy Spirit!

QUESTIONS

Do it God's way, you live; do it your own way, you die. Present some examples where the God's way is followed and where it is not.

Why does being focused and faithful to God matter?

Do our feelings, our image and our physical needs being met provide the best life has to offer or is there something even better; if so, what?

'Actions speak louder than words' is illustrated by Jesus' parable of the two sons required to do a job. One said, 'I will,' and didn't. The other said, 'I will not,' and did. How should life be lived by those who say yes to Jesus?

12

Will You Share Your Faith With Others?

I FIND MYSELF BURDENED AGAIN BY A DEEP longing to reach the 'lost' with the gospel of Christ. The Lord has brought this home to me time and again. Following through the implications of such a conviction requires pure, unfettered dedication in the search for truth.

What is meant by 'lost' in biblical terms when applied to people? It is a gravely worrying situation to be in, and one that presents a frightening outcome if not addressed.

> *My dear friends, if you know people who have wandered off from God's truth, don't write them off. Go after them. Get them back and you will have rescued precious lives from destruction and prevented an epidemic of wandering away from God.*
>
> *James 5:19 (MSG)*

In chapter 15 of Luke's Gospel we read of the 'lost' as told by Jesus himself in three different parables: the lost sheep; the lost coin; and the classic, the prodigal son. In each story the lost is found, sending celestial celebration to record heights!

The lost son got lost because though he had everything, he went wild and 'wasted everything he had'[50]. Things got so bad he fed on pigs' slop. Reaching rock bottom, he thought of home with safe and secure family. He dragged himself out of the dirt and decided to come clean and own up to his big mistakes to a father who never gave up watching for his homecoming. Robes were exchanged for rags and his dad said, 'My son is here – given up for dead and now alive! Given up for lost and now found!'[51]

I well remember a quarter million people gathered on Brighton beach to hear their pop idol, Fat Boy Slim. In my mind's eye, I saw vast crowds appearing to be out for a 'good time', but many of whom (though they may not have known it) driven by a desperate search for God.

In the lives of so many today is a haunting emptiness, a cold depressing misery, a bulldozer push for money, sex and pleasure. Greed, exploitation, abuse is the currency. The rate of exchange produces no winners. All are losers. The victim carries crippling wounds that attack confidence, rob of security and put peace of mind beyond reach. The exploiter's drive will drive him into the dirt. Satan glamorises anything and everything that is destructive so that it appears desirable, irresistible. The harmless 'apple' may be sweet but it is deadly!

Another memory comes to mind. I was walking through the William Booth College in London and was struck with the advertising poster of welcome to the new session of students called 'Bridge-builders'. What a name!

---

[50] Luke 15:13 (MSG)
[51] Luke 15:32 (MSG)

What a mission – charged with the challenge of establishing a bridgehead into the territory of the Evil One! Their mission: search, find and free the lost! By so doing, they, and all who are tuned into Jesus, follow his example:

> *When he saw the crowds, he [Jesus] had compassion on them, because they were harassed and helpless, like sheep without a shepherd.*
>
> *Matthew 9:36 (NIVUK)*

This level of compassion towards, suffering with and feeling of the pain of the lost is not part of our natural make-up. We are not built that way. Yes, most humans feel for those who suffer, but to feel like Jesus felt is altogether different. Only God's Spirit in us produces a raw yearning and provides the impetus and inspiration to 'go for souls and go for the worst!'[52]

> *Jesus said to his disciples, "There are many people to harvest but only a few workers to help harvest them. Pray to the Lord, who owns the harvest, that he will send more workers to gather his harvest."*
>
> *Matthew 9:37,38 (NCV)*

Here and there the practice of prayer is spreading. Going after God in passionate prayer is God going after us in reverse. It is he, nonetheless, who initiates, ignites, inspires and interprets his ways and will to us. Where the people of God are disciplined, determined and regular in

---

[52] William Booth

their prayer life, the results are staggering. Mind, motive, attitude and will bend and blend to God's will. Like Christ, in the Spirit we long for the lost to come to their senses, come into faith in God like they never thought possible and know the life-changing power of God's Spirit in their lives. 'It is significant that Christian character and compassion,' wrote General Clarence Wiseman, 'thrive most vigorously in the lives of those who seek to lead others to the Lord.'[53]

That seeking, that drive, that deep yearning and compassion, where has it gone? Why should so many years pass us by without feeling pain for the lost? Where are the tears that flowed, the voice that cried and the heart that bled for those far from God? When, as a young man, William Booth sought entrance into the Christian ministry, he wrote, 'I wish to reach the dying and tell of him who is life...' Such was the passion and compassion that gripped this young man.

The story is told of a visitor to Booth's birthplace in Nottingham. Moved to tears by what he saw and read in the museum, he knelt and cried, 'Do it again, Lord, do it again!' He was referring to the explosion of the Christian spiritual revolution of the nineteenth century that swept all before it in a tidal wave of revival. Radical spiritual change occurred in the lives of thousands of people: cured of alcoholism and abuse; delivered from wretched poverty and crippling want; above all, changed from the inside out. Mostly ordinary people, they found themselves grasped by the incredible power of God. Filled with a compassion and

---

[53] *A Burning in my Bones;* McGraw-Hill Ryerson (1979)

daring, they devoted themselves to selfless service and sacrifice for those 'others'. My prayer is a simple one which I'd love you to share: *Lord, 'do it again' in my/our lifetime.* There have been times when I have not given all I should nor been all that God wills for me to be. Perhaps you, like me, can identify with that conviction and make the same confession. Together we cry out with the Psalmist:

> *Restore us again, God our Saviour ... Will you not revive us again that your people may rejoice in you?*
>
> *Psalm 85:4,6 (NIVUK)*

As believers we belong to the body of Christ with a command to go and 'preach the good news'. We are simultaneously disciples (followers) and apostles (sent ones). Each has an obligation, a profound privilege, to live the gospel, feel the gospel and speak the gospel.

At Amsterdam 2000 International Conference of Christian Leaders, which I attended, Dr Billy Jang Hwan Kim, pastor and evangelist broadcaster from Korea, spoke on Motives for Evangelism, in which he listed the lawlessness of our world; the lostness of mankind; and the love of God. Another speaker, Reverend Ulrich Parzany from Germany, focused on the unique gift of the evangelist as someone who is 'determined by the urgency of love for the lost'. Writing to the church at Corinth, Paul says, 'It is because of this solemn fear of the Lord, which is ever present in our minds, that we work so hard to win others.'[54] Ulrich stressed that the evangelist has a 'strong desire to communicate Christ to nonbelievers ... [and] is able to listen and understand what nonbelievers are thinking and feeling in relation to the gospel'.

Most importantly, the evangelist is confirmed by the Holy Spirit to lead people to Christ. As we read in Acts 11:21, 'The Lord's hand was with them, and a great number of people believed and turned to the Lord.'[55] Dr John Stott reminds us that the evangelist's message is Bible-based:

> *Without the Bible the evangelist would have nothing to say, nothing worth listening to and no hope of success. If, however, it is based on the Bible, the evangelist's message has content, authority and power.*

The glorious gospel is not some human invention, but of divine revelation. It focuses on Christ. 'Ignorance of Scripture is ignorance of Christ.'[56] Here's the bit we'd rather not hear: if we, as Christians, are faithful in witnessing for our Lord, crucified and risen, it brings with it a high degree of likelihood that we will suffer for it. The uniqueness, the freeness and the high moral standards of the gospel all arouse the world's hostility.

The Bible is like no other book. Above anything else in the world, it contains within its pages God's revelation of himself, his creation and the life that people should live. It is the rock-bed, resource and route to be followed by all

---

[54] 2 Corinthians 5:11 (TLB)
[55] NIVUK
[56] Jerome

who would live life God's way, the way of life eternal. This Word of God stands sure and solid with an authority of its own. Unrivalled and unsurpassed, it is in short God's living, life-changing Word.

People are restless in their search for freedom and fulfilment. Their words are like those of my once three-year-old granddaughter, when I knew she needed my help but was too young to see it: 'I do it myself, Papa!' Being told is not easy, especially if you think you know best. On a broader basis, the Ten Commandments are fine so long as they're a Cecil DeMille, Hollywood version. That's not the real world for many people. To be told – no, *commanded* – as God lays down instructions in his Word, is a concept at best ignored and at worst fiercely opposed by many. Authority is resisted, even at times hated and regarded as the opposite of freedom. However old or young, most don't like to be told what to do, especially when it clashes with their wants and ways. Those who seek the lost need, firstly, humility. They 'stand amazed in the presence of Jesus'[57] but not for long. Standing gives way to kneeling, and kneeling to fervent passionate prayer where Christ is worshipped. From here comes courage to take our stand and boldly present, in the power of the Spirit, God as Sovereign beyond question. He and he alone has the first and last word over all things!

Those who go after the lost don't require position, prominence or prestige. They do, however, need power – the power that comes from God the Holy Spirit.

---

[57] Charles H. Gabriel (1856-1932); *Salvation Army Song Book;* no.466

God didn't send me out to collect a following for myself, but to preach the Message of what he has done ... And he didn't send me to do it with a lot of fancy rhetoric of my own, lest the powerful action at the centre – Christ on the Cross – be trivialised into mere words...Take a good look, friends, at who you were when you got called into this life. I don't see many of "the brightest and the best" among you, not many influential, not many from high-society families. Isn't it obvious that God deliberately chose men and women that the culture overlooks and exploits and abuses, chose these "nobodies" to expose the hollow pretensions of the "somebodies"? That makes it quite clear that none of you can get by with blowing your own horn before God. Everything that we have – right thinking and right living, a clean slate and a fresh start – comes from God by way of Jesus Christ. That's why we have the saying, "If you're going to blow a horn, blow a trumpet for God."

1 Corinthians 1:17,26-31 (MSG)

Concerning the mayhem, the suffering, the nightmare scenario of September 11 (known as 9/11) when Islamist extremists hijacked four aeroplanes, two of which deliberately targeted the Twin Towers in New York, USA, much has been written. All told, the attacks killed almost three thousand people. Where were you on that tragic day? I was attending a lecture at King's College, London University. When the news hit us, the proceedings were halted. An announcement was made. Prayer was offered. Each made their way home.

Sometime after the event, *Songs of Praise* featured Major George Polarek, Incident Commander of The Salvation Army. He, with many others, threw all they could into emergency relief facing fearlessly the horrific scene of human carnage and destruction. George said, 'Sometimes you wonder where God is. When you arrive and there is nothing but a cloud of dust, the dust disappears and then you are at the feet of debris, two hundred million tonnes of debris. Then he sends you a messenger, an angel, or just a volunteer.' George, deeply troubled by the scene of death and destruction, told how he stood next to a Catholic priest when he posed the ultimate question on suffering: 'Where is God?' Pointing to an army of people helping others, in a sea of carnage and catastrophe, the priest responded, 'George, look over there.' It was a fireman praying with a fireman. 'That's Jesus, that's Jesus,' he said. 'Look over here to your left.' There was a Salvationist praying with a police officer. 'Look, that's Jesus. Don't look at the devastation. Look – open your eyes; this is God in our midst.'

The burden and longing for the lost is something born of God in our hearts. Why? To drive us to passionate longing and prayer for the abandoned in a way we've never done before. To feel the pain. To go as those sent by the Lord of the harvest. To follow the Master into broken places. To weep, to work for the lost. Lord, by your grace, 'speak your Son' through us to the lost!

QUESTIONS

As believers, we have a blue light emergency on our hands to reach the lost with the saving gospel of Christ. If you agree, what must we do? If you disagree, why?

Where does a passion for the lost come from and how should it be translated into the everyday of life?

Do you believe in Christian revival? If so, where lies its source and what is the believer called upon to do?

The Bible is God's inspired Word. It is the rock-bed, resource and route for all who follow Jesus. What is its core message to you and why does the world need to hear it?

Prayer

Oh Father, in the morning of our lives
We come face to face with your precious Word.
We yearn for you to speak to us
That we may know the things that matter.
Help us to search your Word;
Open our eyes to see your majesty and glory;
Erase from our minds all distorted thinking.

Oh God, in whom resides all wisdom
Help us each to study your Word.
Grant to us persistence and perseverance
May we not
   slacken in our efforts,
   be diverted to empty arguments, or
   nurse any form of prejudice
As we search your message and meaning.

Open our eyes to your truth.
Forgive us if we have exchanged you for
   some pet system, or
   respectable sounding theory.
May you humble our hearts
That your will and way becomes ours.

Lord, source of Love,
Let your wisdom shape our lives, that all we
Speak, think, and feel may be

honouring to your name,
profitable to your kingdom,
glorifying to your majesty.

Heavenly Father,
Let the light of your Word shine upon on us.
  Warm our hearts to its precepts;
  turn our minds to its understanding;
  bend our wills to its truth.
May heart, mind and will be adorned by
Your Word

Energise us with the might of your Spirit
That we may
Not only know about our Lord
  but know him;
Not only to learn about the Master
  but walk with him;
Not only to grow in knowledge of our Saviour
  but love him who first loved us!
In the precious name of Jesus we pray.

Amen.

Contact the Author

To contact the author, please write to:

Jim Bryden
c/o Onwards and Upwards Publishers Ltd.
4 The Old Smithy
London Road
Rockbeare
EX5 2EA

Or send an email to:

jamesandhelenbryden@icloud.com

More information about the author can be found
on the book's web page:

*www.onwardsandupwards.org/journey-
of-faith-big-questions*

More Books by Jim Bryden

This book opens up Paul's letter to the Ephesians, with 21 daily readings, explanations and applications, as well as optional short exercises to help you dig deeper into the Word.

ISBN: 978-1-78815-717-9
RRP: £6.99

Learn more about the life of Jesus – who he was, what he did and his death and resurrection – with sixteen daily readings, explanations and applications, as well as optional short exercises to help you dig deeper into the Word.

ISBN: 978-1-78815-706-3
RRP: £6.99

Learn more about God's plan to reach the world through the Church, the Body of Christ. Jim shows how we are called to live out our lives and share the gospel with perseverance and faithfulness, with the promise of a heavenly reward.

ISBN: 978-1-78815-557-1
RRP: £6.99

This book tackles many of the difficult questions concerning suffering. How can a good God allow people to suffer? Does God experience our pain? What is the purpose of suffering in the life of a Christian?

ISBN: 978-1-78815-564-9
RRP: £6.99